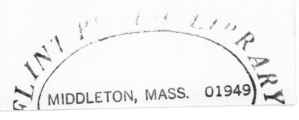

I Speak for the Women

I Speak for the Women

A Story about Lucy Stone

by Stephanie Sammartino McPherson
illustrations by Brian Liedahl

A Carolrhoda Creative Minds Book

Carolrhoda Books, Inc./Minneapolis

To my daughters, Jennifer and Marianne

The author wishes to thank Elinor Rice Hays; Little, Brown and Company; and the Oberlin College Archives, Oberlin, Ohio.

Library of Congress Cataloging-in-Publication Data

McPherson, Stephanie Sammartino.
   I speak for the women : a story about Lucy Stone / by Stephanie Sammartino McPherson ; illustrations by Brian Liedahl.
      p.   cm.—(A Carolrhoda creative minds book)
   Includes bibliographical references.
   Summary: Chronicles the life of the outspoken nineteenth-century supporter of women's rights.
   ISBN 0-87614-740-6
   1. Stone, Lucy, 1818-1893—Juvenile literature. 2. Suffragettes—United States—Biography—Juvenile literature. [1. Stone, Lucy, 1818-1893. 2. Suffragettes. 3. Feminists.] I. Liedahl, Brian, ill. II. Title. III. Series.
JK1899.S8M37   1992
324.6'23'092—dc20
[B]   92-13786
                                                            CIP
                                                             AC

Manufactured in the United States of America

1   2   3   4   5   6   97   96   95   94   93   92

Table of Contents

Introduction

On August 12, 1818, a sudden downpour sent a Massachusetts farmer racing across a field. Francis Stone summoned every man he could find to help save the hay.

His wife, Hannah, watched them splash through the meadows. She was expecting her eighth baby any moment and was sorry to be left alone. Before the men returned that night, the tired mother had to milk the family's eight cows.

The next day, Hannah's daughter Lucy was born. "Oh dear!" sighed Hannah. "I am sorry it is a girl. A woman's life is so hard." She was thinking of much more than milking cows.

She was also thinking of a workday that began before dawn and lasted long after the sun set. Often Francis invited his friends to the farm without asking his wife. Hannah had to cook and do laundry for all the guests as well as for her own large family.

Almost like a child, Hannah was expected to obey her husband in all matters. If she needed new shoes or a bag of sugar, she had to ask Francis for the money. She took care of the children, but he was the one who made almost all the important decisions concerning their futures.

Like most women of her time, Hannah Stone rarely questioned her husband's authority. But Lucy, as she grew up, questioned almost everything about women's roles. She hated to see her mother so tired and meek. Why couldn't her mother stand up for herself? Why didn't her views on important issues count? When Lucy did not get satisfactory answers to questions like these, she determined to do something about it.

1

A Hard Worker

Young Lucy Stone forced her way deeper into the tangled vines at the forest's edge. Her bare feet were dirty and scratched. The tips of her fingers were stained with juice. But the bottom of her basket was covered with plump, ripe berries. Swiftly she reached for more. She needed many more berries to pay for her schoolbooks.

It would be easy to sell her harvest, Lucy decided as she popped a blackberry into her mouth. It would not have been easy, she knew, to convince her father to buy the books. Francis Stone was willing to buy school supplies for his sons. But he hated to spend money on books for a girl.

Many people shared his attitude. In the nineteenth century, women could not vote and rarely owned property. They did not receive as much schooling as their brothers. It was unheard of for a woman to attend college. Needlework and household tasks were considered much more important than higher education.

Lucy did not really mind earning the money for her books. But she did mind very much when her father ignored her dreams. It was very important to Lucy to learn Greek, Latin, and Hebrew. If she studied these languages, she would be able to read the Bible in its original versions. People were always quoting the Bible to prove that women should be silent and obedient in all matters. Lucy wanted to show that their interpretation was wrong. Then maybe men like her father would take the education of their daughters seriously.

To study languages and the other subjects she wanted to learn, Lucy would have to go to college. This was something no American woman had done. "Is the child crazy?" cried Francis Stone when he learned what Lucy wanted to do.

But Lucy had her own doubts about a world that automatically put girls in second place. Sometimes she compared herself to her older brother Luther. Lucy was a faster learner and a harder worker than he was. Why was it crazier for her to go to school than for Luther?

Lucy was so eager for knowledge that she would read almost anything. One day she was seated quietly at her bench in school when she heard the stagecoach approach. Swiftly Lucy's eyes darted to the window. Sometimes the stagecoach passengers tossed out loosely bound reading materials for the children to find. When Lucy saw a shower of papers flutter to the ground, she became so excited that she jumped out the window to pick them up. That night she would have plenty to read when the family gathered around the fireplace.

Lucy liked to watch the great crackling fires her father built after dark. Sometimes she roasted apples or popped corn. And when the neighborhood blacksmith visited, she listened to his stories about wolves, bears, and Indians. At these times, Lucy felt close to her parents and to her brothers and sisters, Francis, Bowman, Eliza, Rhoda, Luther, and Sarah. Lucy especially looked up to Rhoda, a teacher who valued education as highly as Lucy did.

As a farm child, Lucy had many responsibilities. When she was very small, she sat beneath her mother's loom and handed up thread as Hannah did the weaving. Later she learned to make shoes with her sisters. The girls took their shoes to the local store, where the owner gave them four cents a pair in credit. But Lucy's own feet were bare when she and her brother Luther walked the cows to pasture before dawn. Francis Stone was more concerned with the family's good credit than he was with his daughter's comfort.

By the time she was twelve, Lucy had become very concerned about her mother. Constant work and fatigue were beginning to affect Hannah Stone's health. Lucy knew that doing the family's laundry was the hardest job of all. She decided to take over the backbreaking chore for her mother. Every Monday she rose early to complete the first part of the task before school. In 1830 washing clothes meant pumping water to fill the washtub, scrubbing and wringing out each garment separately, and hanging everything to dry in the sunshine. At lunchtime Lucy walked a mile home to take in the clothes. Then she hurried back to school for the afternoon.

Lucy's round face usually glowed from fresh air and exercise, but now she began to look pale and tired like her mother. But she never let her parents know just how weary she felt. She did not want to worry her mother. And she knew her father would rather she cut back on schoolwork than on housework.

Lucy was determined to succeed in both tasks. Fueled by her anger and her sense of injustice, she worked morning and night. Whether it was washing clothes or proving that girls could learn everything that boys did, she never lost sight of her goals.

One day a visitor who believed as Lucy did came to the sewing circle at Lucy's church. Mary Lyon's gown was badly outdated. Her hat was an oddly shaped turban. But as Lucy listened, she forgot all about the speaker's appearance. Mary Lyon wanted to start a new school, Mount Holyoke Female Seminary, where women would study the same subjects as men.

With mounting excitement, Lucy listened to the wonderful idea. If only Mary Lyon could make her dream come true! None of the other girls' schools Lucy knew about offered such an ambitious course of study.

Lucy believed that a good education would give her the skills she needed to help change the world. She would study history and languages. She would show that women could make valuable contributions to society.

It wasn't just women that she wanted to help, however. She also cared deeply about the rights of black people. Although slavery was still legal in the southern United States, a few brave individuals were fighting to abolish it nationwide. They were called abolitionists, and they often faced hostility. Lucy and her family supported the abolitionists. They believed in freedom for everyone.

A deacon in Lucy's church shared the Stones' beliefs. But when he openly joined in antislavery activities, many people became upset. Finally the minister called several meetings to discuss the situation.

At one meeting, the minister asked all those who supported the deacon to raise their hands. Lucy had recently become a full church member. Immediately her hand shot up. She did not notice that none of the other women in the church raised their hands.

The minister's face became serious as he noticed Lucy. "Don't you count her," he ordered his helper. The words burned themselves into Lucy's mind.

The man counting the votes turned to look at Lucy. "Isn't she a member?" he asked.

The minister's reply was swift and scornful. "Yes, but she is not a voting member."

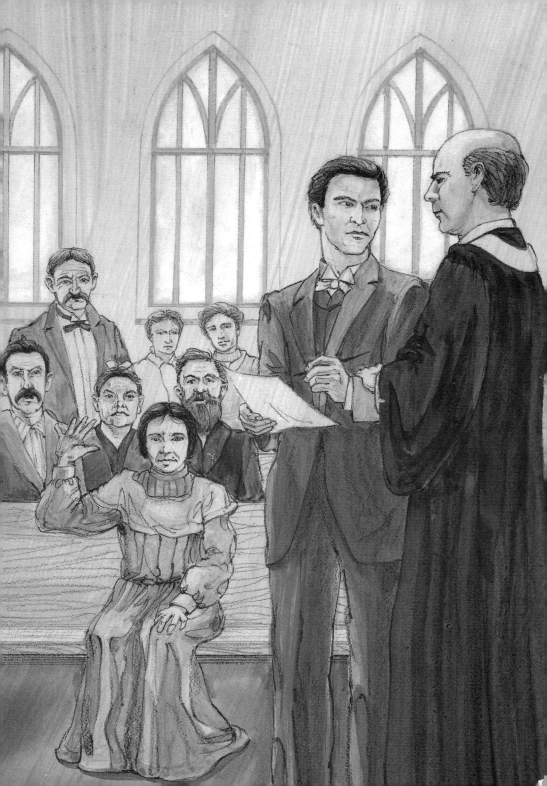

More votes were taken. Each time Lucy's hand was ignored. By the end of the meeting, she was bursting with indignation for herself and for the brave young deacon who had been expelled from the church.

Lucy never forgot what it was like to be denied her vote. Years later she still spoke of "that one uncounted hand." Would there ever come a day when women's votes did count? Maybe if she studied and learned more, Lucy could make that day come sooner.

Her father had very different ideas. He wanted her to quit school and help at home until she married. Lucy proposed instead that she become a teacher like Rhoda.

At first Francis Stone was skeptical. But in the end, his thriftiness won out. If Lucy earned her own money, he would not have to support her anymore.

When she was sixteen, Lucy began her new career. Like most young teachers, she went to board with a family near her first teaching job. Lucy's youngest students in the one-room schoolhouse were six years old. The oldest were almost her own age. But she was able to interest and challenge them all. Students liked her gentle ways. Parents liked the progress their children made. Lucy came to be known as a fine teacher.

As her reputation grew, Lucy was invited to teach at larger schools. Her salary went up to sixteen dollars a month. Although this was high pay for a woman, Lucy knew a man could expect to earn much more.

One winter, students in Paxton, Massachusetts, were stuck. The town's teacher had left after some big boys threw him out of the schoolhouse window into a snowdrift.

Lucy was hired to replace this teacher. Perhaps it was her courage that won her pupils over. Perhaps it was her quiet firmness, her kindness, or her enthusiastic lessons. Whatever her secret, the former troublemakers were happy to do almost anything for Lucy. Yet she did not receive as much money as the man who wound up in the snow.

This especially angered the hardworking teacher because she was saving money to go back to school herself. Sometimes she took off short periods from teaching to study at a girls' seminary. But Mary Lyon's school, which had opened in 1837, was the place she really wanted to go. By the time she could afford her tuition and room and board, Lucy was twenty-one years old.

Lucy could hardly wait to begin her classes, but she wanted to do more than study. She also wanted to start spreading her views.

Shortly after her arrival at Mount Holyoke, Lucy began leaving copies of an antislavery newspaper in the library. She hoped her classmates would read the papers and do some serious thinking. But to Lucy's disappointment, Mary Lyon told her that abolitionist papers would not be permitted in the school. The headmistress felt that controversial issues had no place in her curriculum.

Before Lucy found another chance to further her cause, her older sister Rhoda died. Overcome with grief, Lucy went home to comfort her mother. Then she decided not to return to Mount Holyoke. She would save her money for an even greater adventure.

②

Adventures at Oberlin

The ship rolled rhythmically under Lucy's feet as she pushed her carpetbag against two trunks and prepared to lie down on them. It wouldn't be a very comfortable bed, but Lucy was tired enough to sleep anywhere—even on the deck of a ferryboat crossing Lake Erie. Four years had passed since she had left Mount Holyoke Seminary, and she was on her way to another school at last—Oberlin College in Ohio.

The next day, the ferry landed in Cleveland, Ohio. Lucy transferred to a stagecoach for the last part of her long journey. She was far from home, but in 1843 Oberlin was the only college in the country where black and white men and women studied together.

When she had arrived safely, Lucy sat down to write her mother all about her adventures. She told her about the train ride to Lake Erie and the gentleman who had been so surprised to see her studying Greek. She told about leaning against the railing on the ferryboat and counting the magnificent schooners with their large, billowing sails.

By the time Mrs. Stone received the letter, Lucy had already settled into her new and busy routine. When she wasn't in class, she was usually studying or doing housework for the college. The money she earned—three cents an hour—was important as she struggled to make ends meet.

Minutes were as precious as pennies. Sometimes Lucy opened her book on the windowsill so she could study while she washed dishes. Even with her hands full of soapsuds, she could concentrate on Greek verbs.

From morning till night, she rarely had a spare moment. But Lucy always made time to talk about her antislavery views. She was glad to go to a school that admitted black students and was a stop on the Underground Railroad. This was a secret network of brave abolitionists who helped slaves escape to freedom. Oberlin was one of the safe places where former slaves could rest on their way further north, or even settle down.

Because most of the former slaves had no previous education, Oberlin had a special school

to make them ready for more advanced studies. As an experienced teacher, Lucy received a part-time appointment to teach them. The job meant a twelve-and-a-half cent salary and the chance for Lucy to do work that was especially meaningful to her.

But to Lucy's disappointment, her students' enthusiasm did not match her own, at least not in the beginning. Almost as soon as she entered the classroom the first day, she sensed a tension among her students. Finally a tall black man told her what it was. The men in her class felt insulted, he explained. They did not want a woman to be their teacher.

Hiding her own dismay, Lucy spoke to the men as if they were her friends. She explained that the facts were the same no matter who taught them. And she promised to do her best to teach them the reading and mathematics they needed to learn. In spite of themselves, the men liked Lucy and were willing to give her a try. Soon they were very glad they had. Lucy was as inspiring a teacher as ever.

She was also an excellent student. Lucy studied Greek, Latin, composition, and algebra, the same subjects taken by the male students. But there was one thing the men learned that she was not allowed to study—public speaking.

In the mid-nineteenth century, women were not supposed to speak before an audience. Although a few women had already dared to speak out against slavery, they were strongly criticized by men and women alike. Lucy knew she too would be criticized if she decided to become a public lecturer. Nonetheless, after college she hoped to convince listeners all over New England that slavery was wrong.

During her third year in college, Lucy met a new student who sympathized with her views. Antoinette (Nette) Brown soon became Lucy's best friend. The two girls visited each other's rooms and stayed up late at night to talk. They also enjoyed taking walks together.

During one walk, Nette confided her secret hope to become a minister. Lucy stared in amazement. Never in the history of the country had there been a woman minister. It seemed an impossible goal.

One thing was certain, however. If Nette were to succeed, she needed to develop her speaking skills just as much as Lucy did. So together they hatched a daring plan.

Lucy and Nette found a well-hidden spot in the

woods surrounding the campus. They carefully approached a few classmates they felt they could trust. Then they held the first meeting of their secret debate society for women. Standing under the trees, Lucy addressed a small group of fellow rebels. "Not one of us could state a question or argue it in a successful debate," she said.

This was hardly surprising, since girls were taught it was not ladylike to argue. Girls were never given a chance to express their ideas. They were never even told that their ideas mattered.

The girls in Lucy's debate group believed that what they had to say mattered very much. Even when cold weather forced them out of the woods, they found a way to continue debating. All winter they tramped through the snow to the home of an elderly black woman, who promised to keep their secret.

No one outside her group knew what great strides Lucy was making in public speaking. But everyone knew she was an excellent student and a fine writer. When the time came to graduate, she was selected to write an essay for the graduation ceremony. There was only one problem. Male professors were assigned to read out the essays the women wrote.

Angrily Lucy refused to contribute an essay unless she could read it herself. Soon the whole college was in an uproar. Classmates, teachers, and even the college president urged her to reconsider. But other students chosen to write essays also refused, in a show of support for Lucy.

Although it was even rumored that Lucy might not be allowed to graduate if she didn't give in, she stubbornly continued to work on her black graduation dress. Finally the college gave in. Lucy never wrote the essay, but in 1847, she did become the first Massachusetts woman to receive a college degree.

Graduation day was made especially exciting by the presence on campus of Lucy's hero, William Lloyd Garrison. Garrison was the publisher of an antislavery newspaper and one of the best-known abolitionists in the country. As a well-known college abolitionist, Lucy was presented to the controversial visitor. She told him about her plans to speak against slavery and to urge more rights for women. To her delight, Garrison warmly approved her decision.

Lucy wished her parents could share his enthusiasm. In anxious letters, Mrs. Stone wrote of the hardship and disgrace that Lucy would endure as a public speaker. She hoped her daughter would return to teaching. Or perhaps she could spread her ideas by going from door to door. At least it would be more womanly, Hannah Stone said.

But Lucy wanted to change people's ideas about what was womanly. "You would not object, or think it wrong, for a man to plead the cause of the suffering and the outcast;" she wrote to her mother, "and surely the moral character of the act is not changed because it is done by a woman. . . . I expect to plead not for the slave only, but for suffering humanity everywhere. *Especially do I mean to labor for the elevation of my sex.*" Lucy wanted women to experience the same personal freedom and respect that men took for granted.

Hannah Stone still did not understand. She was happy when Lucy returned home. She was grateful for the help Lucy gave her with household chores. But she was very worried about her daughter. Gently Lucy repeated that she had to speak out for her beliefs.

Lucy's brothers, Bowman and Francis, also felt she had a right to be heard. Bowman was a minister. That winter of 1847, he invited Lucy to come speak at his church.

Some members of the congregation must have been shocked to see a woman in the pulpit. With her pink, round cheeks, short, brown hair, and slight figure, Lucy looked almost like a schoolgirl. But she was twenty-nine years old, wise and dedicated far beyond her years.

When Lucy started to speak, her listeners had another surprise. Her voice was one of the most beautiful they had ever heard. In measured, musical tones, Lucy spoke on the topic closest to her heart—women's rights. She talked about the need for more educational opportunities and the rights that should accompany these opportunities. Women should be allowed to speak out in public, to own their property, and to receive equal pay for doing the same job as a man. She told the congregation about herself, her own dreams and struggles and determination. Other women might have felt the same way privately, but no one had dared to express these views publicly. Flushed with excitement, Lucy concluded her talk and sat down. She had just made one of the first women's rights speeches in the United States.

A short time later, Lucy gave a speech closer to home. This time her father was in the audience. Lucy hated to see him looking so sad and ashamed.

Mr. Stone held his head in his hands. He would not lift his eyes from the floor. But perhaps he felt he owed it to Lucy to be there.

Then Lucy began to speak. Without written notes, she relied on the strength of her convictions and the inspiration of the moment to get her through her speech. The audience fell under the spell of her compelling voice and quiet courage. Slowly a change came over Mr. Stone too. By the end of the speech, he was looking at Lucy as if he had never seen her before. He was smiling with pride. Francis Stone never became an active supporter of the women's movement. But Lucy had finally convinced her father that women had the right to be heard.

③

A Courageous Speaker

Using a flat, round pebble as her hammer, Lucy pounded a tack through the poster announcing her speech. From the corner of her eye, she saw a small gang of boys approaching. She heard their rude laughter and jeering comments. Lucy pretended to study the paper she had just attached to the tree.

Closer and closer crept the boys. Lucy knew they were waiting for her to move on so they could tear down her poster. It was a problem she had faced in several other villages.

Lucy had become an official lecturer for the Massachusetts Anti-Slavery Society. From town to town she traveled, in carriages and open carts. In city halls and churches, she spoke with a sincerity and urgency that impressed many of her listeners greatly. But some people were not ready for Lucy's message. They thought the American economy could not survive without slavery. Other people would not listen to Lucy simply because she was female.

When the boys had almost reached her, Lucy turned to greet them. They started in surprise and mumbled an embarrassed reply.

Lucy began to explain why she was giving a speech and how strongly she felt about the subject of civil rights. She told the boys that children their age or even younger could be beaten at the whim of owners. Slaves worked long hours and were forbidden to learn to read. Sometimes slave children were sold and never saw their parents again.

When Lucy finished talking, the boys were silent. Lucy knew they would not try to steal her posters again. She hoped she would be as successful in convincing their parents.

Often Lucy found that grown-ups behaved much worse than the confused children. Once a prayer book was thrown at Lucy as she sat in a front-row pew waiting to give her speech. Another time a raw egg splattered her dress as she calmly continued her speech.

Sneezing broke out in one auditorium when pranksters burned pepper. Lucy's distinct and untroubled voice cut through the noise. And when someone stuck a hose through the window and drenched her with water, Lucy paused only to put on a shawl. It was the middle of winter. She was shivering with cold. But she finished her speech.

As Lucy's family had predicted, their friends and neighbors were scandalized by Lucy's behavior. Some even told her mother how shocked they were. But Hannah Stone would have none of that. She might not have liked Lucy's activities either, but no one else was going to criticize her daughter. Armed with the same arguments Lucy had used on her, Hannah defended a woman's right to speak in public. Over and over again, she championed the unpopular stand, until she realized she was no longer pretending. She really did believe in what Lucy was doing.

Although she worked for an antislavery society, Lucy often talked about women's rights in her speeches too. In Boston there was a famous statue of a woman called *The Greek Slave* by a

sculptor named Hiram Power. Lucy went to see the well-known work. For a long time, she studied the chained woman in silence. Then she began to cry. The statue seemed to stand for so many women. Soon after that Lucy arranged to speak for women's rights during the week and abolition on the weekends.

Many women came up to talk to Lucy after her speeches. They had their own tales of injustice and frustration to share. Lucy sympathized and remembered their stories for future speeches.

Most of Lucy's friends in the antislavery movement, both male and female, were also in favor of women's rights. But the women's movement was not as well organized as the abolitionist cause. Lucy and several other people thought the time had come to change this.

In May of 1850, nine women met after some antislavery talks in Boston. Together they made plans for a national women's rights convention. Two years earlier, a smaller meeting had been held at Seneca Falls, New York, but this was the first time the entire country would be invited to attend. Lucy was the first person to sign the petition calling for the event.

During the summer before the convention, Lucy

came down with typhoid fever. For eighteen days, she lay helpless in a dingy hotel room while her sister-in-law watched over her. By the time she reached home, Lucy was worn out physically and mentally. At first it seemed she could not possibly make it to the convention.

But the thought of not attending such an important event seemed equally impossible to her. The convention was being held in the nearby town of Worcester. Even if she was not up to speaking, Lucy decided, she could at least attend as a spectator.

More than a thousand people were jammed into the hall when the convention opened on October 23. Among the many speakers were William Lloyd Garrison, Antoinette Brown, and black abolitionists Sojourner Truth and Frederick Douglass. Lucy felt inspired to be surrounded by such brave individuals. Unable to remain silent after all, she gave one of the most stirring speeches of the convention.

To some men and women, the new ideas of female equality seemed strange and threatening. They thought that family life would suffer if women demanded educational and business opportunities. Other people felt challenged and excited by the speakers' ideas. They saw the justice of the new women's movement.

Although many reporters attended the convention, few recognized it for the historic event it was. One newspaper referred to the participants as a "gathering of crazy old women" and "fugitive lunatics." Other journalists called the meeting a "hen convention." But *The New York Tribune* supported the women's movement and published a fine summary of Lucy's speech.

One *Tribune* reader was especially struck with Lucy's words. Susan B. Anthony decided the time had come for her to fight for women's rights too. Soon she was as hardworking and dedicated as anyone in the movement. Lucy and Susan became good friends. They exchanged letters and met at conventions. They talked about every issue that touched women's lives.

And they encouraged each other in a daring fashion experiment. The two women wore bloomers, a newly invented garment that consisted of baggy pants gathered at the ankle and worn under a skirt. Lucy liked bloomers for the freedom and comfort they provided. The elaborate long dresses and stiff petticoats most women wore were awkward and restricted movement.

But bloomers had their drawbacks. When Lucy first started wearing them, some antislavery speakers were even afraid to invite her to conventions. They thought that her unusual costume would overshadow what she had to say. After several speeches, Lucy proved that people would listen to her no matter what she wore.

In spite of the fuss and laughter, Lucy hoped to liberate women from fashion. Comfort and practicality should be just as important as style, she thought. To emphasize her point, she wore bloomers in 1852 to the Third National Women's Rights Convention in Syracuse, New York. Some people must have found her message as strange as her outfit. Women should not pay taxes, she declared. Then she repeated the same argument that the American colonists had used against England during the Revolutionary War. Taxation without representation was unfair, the colonists had decided. Lucy said that women, like the colonists, were not represented, because they had no voice in making the taxes or saying how the money should be used.

From meeting to meeting, Lucy crisscrossed the countryside, making speeches. She was earning her own living. She was speaking out against injustice and proving that women deserved to be treated seriously. But sometimes Lucy thought there was something missing in her life. Sometimes she wondered what it would be like to be married and have children.

Dutifully Lucy tried to ignore these dreams. When a woman married, she lost what few rights she did have. Her husband controlled all her property and was the sole legal guardian of the children. "I shall not be married ever," Lucy wrote to Nette. "I have not yet seen the man whom I have the slightest wish to marry, and if I had it will take longer than my lifetime for the obstacles to be removed which are in the way of a married woman having any being of her own."

4

A Marriage
ahead of Its Time

Lucy was back at home during a break in her busy lecturing schedule. Standing on the kitchen table, clad comfortably in bloomers, she stretched and swept her paintbrush back and forth across the ceiling.

Suddenly there was a knock at the back door. A good-looking young man with a bushy black beard was standing on the doorstep. He smiled and introduced himself as Henry Blackwell.

Recently Henry had heard Lucy speak at antislavery meetings in Boston and New York. Henry also reminded her about their first meeting, when she had stopped at his hardware store in Cincinnati. He had deeply admired the brave young woman who was taking her brother's widow back to Massachusetts to live. Even after several years, he could not get Lucy out of his mind.

Lucy found herself liking Henry very much too. He believed in the same causes as she did. Like Lucy, Henry felt women should have all the educational opportunities that men did. He was proud of his sister Elizabeth, the first woman in the United States to graduate from medical school.

Henry was earnest, polite, and full of interesting conversation. He even offered to whitewash the ceiling for Lucy. Instead Lucy allowed him to help peel potatoes. She invited him to stay for dinner and introduced him to her parents.

After dinner Lucy took Henry for her favorite walk, to the top of Coy's Hill. Soon she discovered the real reason for his visit. Henry wanted to marry her.

Surprised and deeply moved, Lucy listened to his proposal. Henry was nothing like her previous suitors. For an instant, he made almost anything seem possible. Then Lucy explained that she could not marry anyone. She said she was too busy with

her lecturing career and too angry at a legal system that favored husbands over wives.

Henry understood her reasons, but he did not give up. He wrote to Lucy several days after his visit, and Lucy wrote back. They began to look forward to each other's letters. That October they met again at Niagara Falls. Then they traveled to Cleveland, Ohio, where the Fourth National Women's Rights Convention was being held. While Lucy listened with delight, Henry gave his first speech urging equal rights for women.

Henry helped Lucy plan a lecturing route in the Midwest. For part of her tour, she stayed with the Blackwell family in Cincinnati. She came to be very fond of Henry's mother and sisters. And she felt herself more and more drawn to Henry himself. But Lucy was still not ready for marriage. And she worried because Henry was seven years younger than she was.

Henry told her the difference in their ages did not matter. When Lucy continued her lecturing tour, he continued to write to her. They saw each other whenever they could.

The next summer, Lucy received a letter that filled her with pride. Henry told her all about his rescue of an eight-year-old slave girl traveling by train through Ohio. He had boarded the train in Salem, Ohio, and asked the girl if she wanted to be free. When she said yes, he lifted her from her seat and quickly hustled her off the train. According to state law, slaves brought into Ohio by their owners were granted immediate freedom. All they had to do was state their wishes on the matter. Her former owners protested loudly, but there was nothing they could do.

Lucy could not stop thinking about Henry's courage. She longed to see him in person. When she finally got her wish, she agreed to become Henry's wife.

On May 1, 1855, Lucy and Henry were married in her parents' home. The sparkling parlor decorated with flowers looked like the setting of any small country wedding. But this was no ordinary ceremony. Before they exchanged vows, Henry held Lucy's hand and read a protest against the marriage laws that made women second-class citizens.

"We believe that personal independence and equal human rights can never be forfeited, except for crime," said Henry. "That marriage should be an equal and permanent partnership, and so recognized by law."

After their wedding, Lucy and Henry were equal partners in every way. Lucy continued to travel and lecture. Henry was often away on business. But they cherished the time they spent together at the Blackwell family home in Cincinnati.

When they had been married a year, Lucy and Henry set off by horse and buggy to Bad Axe County, Wisconsin, where Henry owned some land. During their two-month stay in Viroqua, Wisconsin, Henry surveyed the land they owned, and Lucy got a close-up look at the lot of pioneer women. She was appalled at the hardships they endured and the way the men took their services for granted. At once she began spreading her own ideas about freedom.

On July 4, 1856, Lucy gave a speech to celebrate Independence Day. Surrounded by sun-browned pioneers, she stood on a wooden platform to deliver her message of equal rights.

Suddenly Lucy found herself sitting in the dirt among planks of splintered wood. The rough stage had given way under her. Her hands were bruised, and her legs smarted, but she wasn't hurt. Quickly she rose from the rubble and brushed off her dress. "So will this country fall unless slavery is abolished!" she told the startled audience.

After their summer in Viroqua, Lucy and Henry headed east and lived for a time with Henry's sisters, Doctors Elizabeth and Emily Blackwell, in New York. The home in Ohio had recently been sold, so Mrs. Blackwell and another daughter, Marian, had already moved in.

To Lucy's delight, her old friend Nette lived in the house too. Shortly after Lucy's own marriage, Nette had married Henry's brother Sam. The two friends now considered themselves sisters. Lucy, who loved children, liked to help care for Nette's baby daughter.

But Lucy did not share a name with her old friend. A year after her marriage, she dropped the word Blackwell from her name. Some people found this confusing. No woman in the United States had ever done this before. Occasionally she was accused of not being really married. But Henry understood and supported her completely.

Although some progress had been made in women's rights, Lucy knew much more needed to be done. She kept traveling and lecturing. She was also looking for a house that she and Henry could call their own. In the spring of 1857, they found a home surrounded by fruit trees in Orange, New Jersey.

That summer Lucy rested at home while Henry continued his business trips for a company that published agricultural books. He returned home shortly before Lucy gave birth to a baby girl on September 14. The happy parents named her Alice Stone Blackwell.

As the months passed, Alice grew into a demanding, active youngster. Lucy no longer felt free to continue her campaigns. After taking her eight-month-old daughter to the Women's Rights Convention of 1858, she did very little speaking and concentrated on being a mother.

Susan B. Anthony was bitterly disappointed. She begged Lucy to return to public life. Lucy longed to do more, but she felt too tied down to resume her old activities. "I wish I felt the old impulse and power to lecture," she wrote Nette in 1859. But when she looked at her sleeping daughter, she knew "... that for these years I can only be a mother."

Susan B. Anthony, Elizabeth Cady Stanton, and others continued to lecture and fight for women's rights until the Civil War began, one year later. During the war, people were too concerned with bloodshed and battles to spare much thought for the women's movement.

5

The Fight for Woman Suffrage

As president of the Women's National Loyal League, Lucy stood before an audience once more. She was forty-five years old, and years of hard work were beginning to take their toll. Her face was etched with fine lines. Her figure had grown stout and matronly. But her voice was as youthful and musical as ever as she addressed the women before her. "If the right of one single human being is to be disregarded by us, we fail in our loyalty to the country," she declared.

Although the Civil War was being fought to free the slaves, slavery was still legal in some states. The Women's National Loyal League had been founded by Susan B. Anthony and Elizabeth Cady Stanton to pressure Congress for a constitutional amendment to end slavery.

Women all over the Union gathered one hundred thousand signatures on petitions calling for the end of slavery. In 1865 Congress passed the Thirteenth Amendment, which abolished slavery in the United States. Women still could not vote, but they had helped shape history.

In some ways, women made great strides during the Civil War. Some women took over the jobs of men who had gone off to fight. Others organized fund-raisers or became nurses. They learned to believe in themselves and to voice their opinions openly. Many women began to realize that they could make important contributions to society outside the home.

But when the war ended in 1865, few people turned their thoughts to women's rights. All abolitionists, both men and women, wanted to secure black men the right to vote. But the men were afraid that if women pressed for the vote at the same time, both measures would fail. This is the black man's hour, they said over and over. Women would simply have to wait.

Lucy did not want to wait. During the Civil War, she had led a quiet life in New York. She did volunteer work for the Loyal League, rolled bandages, and looked after her daughter. But at eight years old, Alice no longer required her mother's constant care. Lucy knew the time had come to return to public speaking.

In January of 1866, Lucy and Susan B. Anthony helped found the American Equal Rights Association in Boston. Its aim was to achieve voting rights for black and white women and black men. One year later, Lucy had resumed her vigorous travel schedule. In March she spoke to the New Jersey state legislature. Then she and Henry settled Alice in for a long visit with her aunt Elizabeth and headed off for Kansas. For the first time, voters were being asked to consider black and woman suffrage. If enough Kansas men voted in favor of suffrage, black citizens and women in that state would gain the right to vote.

For three months, Lucy and Henry jolted over the prairie state in carriages and open wagons. They spoke in schools, churches, and even stores. One time they were caught in a sudden storm that

plastered their clothes to their bodies and turned the ground to mud before their eyes. Lucy caught a terrible cold. Henry felt that her voice never regained its former strength. But she continued to raise that voice whenever there was anyone to listen.

Even when both issues were defeated, Lucy believed that success was not far off. Over nine thousand men had voted in favor of woman suffrage. Surely that was a hopeful beginning. And in the meantime, a constitutional amendment that would give all black men the right to vote would soon be considered before Congress. Lucy was distressed that the proposed amendment did not include women too. It seemed hard to support an amendment giving others the right to vote when she still couldn't vote herself. But after much inner debate, Lucy decided to support the amendment. She and Henry felt it was a step in the right direction.

Susan B. Anthony and Elizabeth Cady Stanton took the opposite side. They refused to work for an amendment that did not give women their long-overdue rights.

Lucy's disagreements with the other two leaders became so serious that they could no longer work together. Many women supported Lucy's position. Others agreed with Susan B. Anthony. In 1869 Susan and Elizabeth quietly formed their own organization, the National Woman Suffrage Association. Taken by surprise, Lucy and Henry felt that they had been purposely excluded from the proceedings. They responded later that year by establishing the American Woman Suffrage Association.

Suddenly Lucy was busier than ever. The family moved to Boston, and she set about establishing a newspaper to promote the ideas of the new organization. Named *The Woman's Journal*, it covered everything from household hints to education to suffrage news. Now there was money to be raised, stories to be written, and research to be done. For a while, Lucy and Henry set up housekeeping in cramped rooms over the newspaper's office.

But after years of moving around, Lucy was anxious to settle down. In 1870, she and Henry bought a large house in Boston. Lucy fell in love with the beautiful view at once. From the porch, she could see Boston Harbor, Dorchester Bay, and the Neponset River.

Although Lucy was aging and sometimes in poor

health, she rarely allowed hard work to get her down. In spite of all its problems, *The Woman's Journal* thrived. Some of the best writers in the nation contributed articles. Women from Maine to California subscribed. And as the years passed, more and more doves began to appear on the pages. A picture of a dove with an olive branch was used to illustrate any victory for woman suffrage.

In 1879 a dove appeared in the paper when Massachusetts women were given the right to vote for school committee members. For the first time in her sixty years, a jubilant Lucy went to register to vote. But to her dismay, her registration as Lucy Stone was cancelled. Only if she signed her name "Mrs. Henry Blackwell" would she be allowed to vote. It was a bitter moment for Lucy. As much as she yearned to vote, her own name meant too much to her to abandon it.

More determined than ever, Lucy continued her work. School elections were only the beginning. States now also had the power to grant women suffrage in city, state, and national elections. Lucy and Henry believed that when enough states took action, the federal government would have to act too. Though *The Woman's Journal* spread their views all over the country, Lucy and Henry also felt a need to get out and actively campaign when suffrage questions were put before the public. Through the years, many new audiences throughout the country discovered that Lucy was a persuasive and powerful speaker.

But there was one place Lucy never expected to speak. Almost forty years later, she still remembered her anger at not being allowed to read her graduation essay at Oberlin. Now the school was celebrating its fiftieth anniversary, and to her surprise, Lucy was invited to be a guest speaker.

Lucy returned to her old college with Henry and Nette. She was sixty-five years old, and while she had grown old, the campus had grown up. It was filled with new buildings. Trees had been planted in the once-empty fields. But these changes weren't nearly as important as the change in attitude, Lucy decided.

On July 4, 1883, Lucy sat on the speaker's platform and watched the flag snapping in the breeze. She thought of thousands of other flags flying across the nation. When the time came for her to speak, she reminded her listeners that these flags were flying "over twenty millions of women who are taxed without representation and governed without their consent." She urged the college

to do everything possible to secure women the right to vote.

Lucy continued to do everything in her power too. She kept on writing, editing, traveling, and speaking. And when she realized that a joining of the two suffrage organizations was in the best interest of their cause, she put aside her personal feelings. Alice, now a young woman as dedicated to woman suffrage as her parents were, took the lead in bringing the two groups together. On December 21, 1887, Susan B. Anthony and her assistant Rachel Foster arrived at the office of *The Woman's Journal* to speak with Lucy and Alice. The two groups agreed to merge their organizations and to work toward a constitutional amendment for woman suffrage. (The Fifteenth Amendment had already given black men the right to vote.) Although some personal bitterness still existed between the older women, Lucy felt this merger was an important step in the battle for suffrage.

Often tired and troubled by health problems, Lucy continued her work. She felt weak and was suffering from a stomach ailment when she spoke at the Chicago World's Fair in 1893. Most of the women in the audience were younger than Lucy. Many looked upon her as a pioneer and a heroine.

Lucy counted on these young women to win political equality at last. She was glad to feel that she had done her part to make their job easier.

Lucy had insisted on her right to an education. She had braved scorn and ridicule to protest injustice. And she had spent years writing and editing a newspaper for women. With all the feeling and eloquence of her earlier speeches, Lucy told her audience how thankful she was "that the young women of today do not and can never know at what price their right to free speech and to speak at all in public has been earned."

Afterword

After Lucy died in 1893, a heartbroken Henry told Alice, "We must try to keep Mamma's flag flying."

And they did. For many years Alice and Henry continued to edit the newspaper and work for woman suffrage. When Henry died in 1909, Alice carried on alone.

Finally, in 1920, the Nineteenth Amendment guaranteed women the right to vote. Most of the original suffragists had died by then. But Alice remembered her mother's ceaseless activity and unconquerable faith. And Antoinette Brown Blackwell, who had participated in the first National Woman's Rights Convention, lived to cast her first and only ballot at the age of ninety-five. These dedicated crusaders knew that no one had worked harder than Lucy Stone to make their present triumph possible.

Bibliography

Books:

Blackwell, Alice Stone. *Lucy Stone, Pioneer of Women's Rights.* Boston: Little, Brown and Company, 1930.

Buhle, Mari Jo and Paul. *The Concise History of Woman Suffrage: Selections from the Classic Work of Stanton, Anthony, Gage, and Harper.* Urbana, Illinois: University of Illinois Press, 1978.

Flexner, Eleanor. *Century of Struggle: The Woman's Rights Movement in the United States.* Cambridge, Massachusetts: The Belknap Press of Harvard University Press, 1959.

Hays, Elinor Rice. *Morning Star, A Biography of Lucy Stone.* New York: Harcourt, Brace, and World, Inc., 1961

Hays, Elinor Rice. *Those Extraordinary Blackwells: The Story of a Journey to a Better World.* New York: Harcourt, Brace, and World, Inc., 1967.

Lasser, Carol, and Marlene Deahl Merrill, eds. *Soulmates: The Oberlin Correspondence of Lucy Stone and Antoinette Brown Blackwell, 1846-1850.* Oberlin, Ohio: Oberlin College, 1983.

Lasser, Carol, and Marlene Deahl Merrill, eds. *Friends and Sisters: Letters Between Lucy Stone and Antoinette Brown Blackwell, 1846-1893.* Urbana, Illinois: University of Illinois Press, 1987.

Wheeler, Leslie, ed. *Loving Warriors, Selected Letters of Lucy Stone and Henry B. Blackwell, 1853-1893.* New York: The Dial Press, 1981.

Articles:

Hosford, Francis J., Associate Professor Emeritus. "The Pioneer Women of Oberlin College: IV. Lucy Stone." *The Oberlin Alumni Magazine* (February 1927). (Courtesy of Oberlin College Archives.)

Stone, Lucy. "Oberlin and Woman." From *Oberlin Jubilee.* (Courtesy of Oberlin College Archives.)

"Memorial Number of Mrs. Lucy Stone." *The Woman's Journal,* October 28, 1893.

Other sources include various books, journal articles, and biographical dictionaries.